William Cornelius Reichel, Maurice Charles Jones

A Red Rose from the Olden Time

William Cornelius Reichel, Maurice Charles Jones

A Red Rose from the Olden Time

ISBN/EAN: 9783337258078

Printed in Europe, USA, Canada, Australia, Japan

Cover: Foto ©Thomas Meinert / pixelio.de

More available books at **www.hansebooks.com**

A Red Rose from the Olden Time;

or,

A Ramble Through The Annals

OF THE

ROSE INN,

ON THE BARONY OF NAZARETH,

IN THE DAYS OF THE PROVINCE:

BASED ON

"The Old Inns at Nazareth."

A PAPER,

READ AT THE CENTENARY OF THE "NAZARETH INN,"

JUNE 9th, 1871,

By MAURICE C. JONES,

OF BETHLEHEM, PENNA.

PHILADELPHIA:

KING & BAIRD, PRINTERS, 607 SANSOM STREET.

1872.

"**Released and Confirmed** unto the said Letitia Aubrey her Heirs and Assigns for evermore,—but **to be holden** of John Penn Thomas Penn and Richard Penn their Heirs and Assigns in free and common Soccage as of the Seigniory of Windsor on **yielding and paying** therefor to the said John Penn Thomas Penn and Richard Penn their Heirs and Assigns **ONE RED ROSE** on the twenty-fourth Day of June yearly if the same shall be demanded in full for all Services Customs and Rents."

Deed 25 Sept. 1731.

JOHN PENN *et al.* to

MRS. LETITIA AUBREY

Release in Fee of 5,000 Acres of Land in Pennsilvania.

1752 — 1871.

The Old Nazareth Inns.

Committee of Arrangements.

JUNE 9th, 1871.

CHAIRMAN,

THOMAS SPARKS.

SECRETARY,

PHILIP A. CREGAR.

JAMES HENRY,	WILLIAM, H. JORDAN,
Capt. WILLIAM MAN,	JOHN THOMAS,
EDWARD O. SMITH,	RICHARD M. SHOEMAKER,
GEORGE A. KOHLER,	FRANK HOWELL ELLIS.

2

ON the occasion of a dinner at the Nazareth Inn on the 9th of June last,—commemorative of the centennial anniversary of that notable house of entertainment,—Maurice C. Jones, of Bethlehem, read a brief but highly interesting paper on its history, and on the history of its predecessor, "The Rose." The essay met with the unqualified approbation of the company, and the wish being simultaneously expressed that it might be published at an early day, the editor was requested to extend Dr. Jones' researches, so as to be enabled to perfect as nearly as possible the picture, whose forms in outline had been so happily conceived.

Such is, in brief, the origin of "A Red Rose from the Olden Time;" for whose historical element the reader is largely indebted to the venerable antiquary, Mr. Andrew G. Kern of Nazareth, and to James Henry, of Bolton on Lehietan, President of the Moravian Historical Society.

THE EDITOR.

BETHLEHEM, 4th Jan. of 1872.

A Red Rose from the Olden Time.

1752.

HAT charming tract of rolling country, rich in springs and water-courses, rich in meadows and rich in wheat-growing lands, which lies in the very heart of Northampton County, being embraced within the limits of Upper Nazareth township, was purchased by the Moravians in the summer of 1741. Its contents, we are told, were five thousand acres, every acre being measured and computed according to the dimensions of acres, mentioned and approved in and by the statute made in the thirty-third year of the reign of King Edward the First. After the founding of Bethlehem, the Moravians made successive improvements on this tract,—at Ephrata in 1743, at Old

Nazareth in 1744, at Gnadenthal in 1745, at Christian's Spring in 1748, and at Friedensthal in 1749; and here they lived, somewhat after the manner of the primitive Christians, in an Economy. Thus happy years and halcyon days rolled on, when, in 1751, there came orders from the head-men of the Church in the old country, for the laying out of a village on some eligible spot within the limits of this princely domain, like unto the Moravian villages in Germany. Bishop Spangenberg, accordingly, selected and had surveyed into a town-plot a parcel of one hundred and sixty acres, adjacent to the northeastern boundary of the modern borough of Nazareth. This survey was commenced on the third day of January, 1752; preparations were, at the same time, set on foot for the erection of needed dwellings on the opening of spring, and the name of Gnadenstadt was given to the projected town. But the inhabitants of Nazareth, whom it was proposed transferring thither, could not be prevailed upon to exchange the poetry of an Economy for the prose of town-life and the restrictions of a municipium. Hence the building of Gnadenstadt was indefinitely postponed and abandoned, save that a frame-building of two stories, which had assumed dimensions (its foundation-stone having been laid on the 27th of March), while the people of Nazareth were demurring in the face of the head-men and the Bishop, was, some time after their final decision, fully completed.* This building was the first house of entertainment on the tract, or on "the Barony," as it was called,—in as far as when William Penn, of Worminghurst, in the County of Sussex, Esq., released and confirmed its five thousand acres to his trusty friend Sir John Fagg, for the sole use and behoof of his beloved daughter Letitia—he confirmed them to him with the privilege of erecting them into one manor, and with the additional privilege of holding thereon court baron and views of frank pledge for the conservation of the peace;—and being, as has been stated, the first house of entertainment erected at Nazareth, and the legitimate predecessor of the house in which we

---

* It should have been stated, that in addition to this " house of enter-tainment erected for strangers and for the conveniency of the workmen," there was another dwelling finished in the spring of 1752. This stood vacant until in May of 1760, when it was occupied by John George and Mary C. Claus. In the autumn of 1761, Gottlieb Demuth (see later in this paper) took up a lot and blocked up a house. In this way the building of Gnadenstadt was gradually resumed, and the place grew; but in June of 1762, it received the name of Schœneck i. e., " Pretty Cor-ner," and in October of the same year, divine worship (for which the in-habitants had met in Claus's house up to that time) was first held in the new school and parsonage. The stone church in the hamlet of Schœn-eck, embowered so charmingly in weeping willows to the very pinnacle of its antique belfry, was completed in 1793, and dedicated on the 20th day of October of that year.

John George Claus, the first inhabitant of Schœneck, was born in Alsace in 1722. He deceased in February of 1763, and his remains were the first that were buried in the graveyard at Schœneck.

are met, it behooves us not to pass it by lightly, but to ponder what of its history has been rescued from oblivion by antiquarian research.

It was in the late summer of 1752, that the ancient caravansary was completed, and, on the 15th day of September, it was occupied by John Frederic Schaub, cooper, and Divert Mary, his faithful wife,— he, the first of a blameless line of publicans.* Standing on the very confines of barbarism, like a beacon off some dark and stormy coast, its cheering presence was henceforth hailed by horsemen and packers journeying on the King's road, that led past, and over the mountain many miles northward, to the farms and settlements that dotted both shores of the Delaware in the Minisinks. For almost twenty years its doors stood invitingly open to weary travellers, who longed for surcease from the toils of the

---

* Mr. Schaub was born in Switzerland in 1717. He and his wife were one of thirty-three Moravian couples, that were brought over from Europe, late in the Autumn of 1743, and settled at Nazareth. About 1747 he made a venture in real estate, taking up two parcels of woodland on the Lehigh Mountain, near Bethlehem, which were patented to him by the three Penns, in October of 1752. These he conveyed to John Okely in December following, and thus they became part of the great Moravian tract surrounding Bethlehem, which tract eventually embraced upwards of 10,000 acres. In 1755, Mr. Schaub removed to Bethabara, the first settlement made by the Moravians on their possessions in what was then Anson County, North Carolina. He deceased at Bethany, a neighboring settlement, in 1801.

way, and for the rest and refreshment of an inn; and for almost twenty years, its hospitable roof sheltered the Brethren, too, who came to visit their Brethren at Nazareth.

In this way *Der neue Gasthof*, as it was modestly called, grew in favor with the race of articulate men; and its achievements having been duly blazoned at the lists far and near, the inn was entitled to wear a coat-of-arms, upon which there appeared on the 6th day of August, 1754, during the incumbency of John F. Schaub, cooper, and Divert Mary, his wife, a full-blown scarlet rose. And hence, and ever afterwards it was known as *Der Gasthof zur Rose,—Die Rose,—* THE ROSE. The origin of this floral emblem and this floral appellation is fortunately a matter of history. They were not bestowed on the lonely hospice because its presence made the surrounding wilderness of scrub-oak and stunted pines to blossom like the queen of flowers; nor because its surcoat was dyed in Spanish brown. They were both commemorative; for when John Penn, Thomas Penn, and Richard Penn, released to Letitia Aubrey, their half-sister, gentlewoman, the five thousand acres that had been confirmed to his trusty friend Sir John Fagg, for her sole use and behoof by William Penn of Worminghurst, in the County of Sussex, Esq., it was done on the condition of the payment of ONE RED ROSE, yearly, for all services, customs and rents.

Soon after this important event in the annals of the inn, a cloud began to gather along the northern horizon of the Province, which, ere the lapse of a twelvemonth, burst in fire and blood. The French and Indians had taken the war-path, and were come down upon the defenceless frontiers. Schaub and Divert Mary, his wife, and their son Johnny (the first child of white parents born at Nazareth), had retired from The Rose (August 14th, 1754); John Nicholas Weinland, farmer and musician, had administered its concerns from that date to the 11th day of December following,—and so it came to pass that the fury of this Indian war fell during the incumbency of Albrecht Klotz, last from Tulpehocken, but a native of Hohenlohe in the Lower Palatinate, blacksmith, and Ann Margaret, née Rieth, born in Scoharie, a daughter of old Michael Rieth, of Tulpehocken, his faithful wife. The following curious document dated at Philadelphia on the 2d of August, 1755, attests that Mr. Klotz assumed the responsibilities of his new trust with the full approbation and sanction of the highest Provincial authority for the time being,—it having been issued by the Honorable Robert Hunter Morris, Esq., Lieutenant Governor of the Province of Pennsylvania and the Counties of New Castle, Kent and Sussex on Delaware. It reads thus:

"Whereas Albrecht Klotz hath been recommended unto me as
"a sober and fit person to keep a house of entertainment, and
"being requested to grant him a license for the same, I do hereby
"license and allow the said Albrecht Klotz to keep a public
"house in the township of Lehigh* in the County of North-
"ampton, for the selling of wine, rum, punch and other spirituous
"liquors, until the 10th day of August next; Provided,. he shall
"not, at any time in the said term, suffer any drunkenness, unlawful
"gaming, or any other disorders, or sell any drink to the Indians
"to debauch or hurt them; but in all things observe and practice
"all laws and ordinances of this Government to his said employ-
"ment relating.

"Given under my hand and seal-at-arms, the 2d day of August,.
"in the Twenty-ninth year of our Sovereign Lord and King
"George the Second, and in the year of our Lord One Thousand
"seven hundred and fifty-five.

[L. s.]   Signed ROBERT H. MORRIS."

It must here be added, that Christian and Anna
Stotz had, in April of 1755, been associated with the
Klotzes at The Rose, to preside over its bureau of
agriculture, and that Joseph, a negro from the Gold

---

* Lehigh township was organized by the Court in September of 1754,
and was defined as extending from the Lehigh River on the west, east-
wards along the foot of the Blue Mountain, to the "old Minisink
Road." At the same time, its adjacents from said road as far the line
of Mount Bethel, received the name of Plainfield. Plainfield township
was organized in 1757. The Rose-farm, in part, at the date of the
above license lay in Lehigh, subsequently in Plainfield, and at a later day
in Bushkill.

Coast, was hostler at the critical juncture to which
the current of this history has drifted.

On the 1st of November, 1755, sixty thousand
persons perished violently in the city of Lisbon, as
it was being shaken to its foundations by the un-
stable earth that reeled like a drunkard in his cups;
and in the early morning of the 18th of November
of the same year, there was heard on the Barony,
with a star-lit sky overhead, a sound as of a rushing
wind and of the booming of distant siege guns,—
when lo! the doors at The Rose swung on their
hinges, and stood open! Thus it is written in the
book of our chronicles—and on its dusty pages it
furthermore stands recorded, that the sleepers at the
inn, on that frosty November morning, rocked in
their beds as do mariners in hammocks out at sea.
It would be presumptuous for the historian to en-
deavor to determine what was the connection between
these far distant occurrences,—so nearly synchronous
and so like in character, although, fortunately for the
inmates of The Rose, unlike in degree and in
effects.

Leaving men of science to conjecture or decide as
they please, we will proceed to state, that seven days
after these ominous forebodings, word was brought
to Nazareth of the surprise and massacre on the
Mahoning,—and on the evening of that seventh day,
upwards of sixty terrified men, women and children

from the adjacents north of the Barony thronged
the doorway of the Moravian inn, clamorous for
shelter and for protection from the murdering
Indians. Among these fugitives were the Clevels*
from the banks of the romantic Bushkill, and the
Stechers (whose seedling apple is in high esteem to
the present day), the Germantons, the Koehlers, the
Klases and the Kostenbaders, all from the plains of
upper Northampton, dwarf-oaked and slaty, and rich
in pheasants and stemless cypripedia.

Such was the beginning of that precipitate evacu-
ation of the frontiers, which culminated subsequent
to the surprise at Frederic Hoeth's and the affair
at Broadhead's ;—there being on the 17th day of
the eventful month of December, 1755, according
to an official enumeration, two hundred refugees
billeted at Nazareth and Ephrata, and one hundred
at the other settlements on the tract. It was as
promiscuous an assemblage as had ever been
gathered in so short a time, embracing men of diverse nationalities and creeds, and women of diverse
tongues. There were the Eisenmanns, the Geislys,
the Hecks, the Hesses, the Heises, the Heimanns,

---

* Francis and George Clevel, sons of Francois and Louise Clevel, née
Fraché, and grandsons of French Protestants who had fled from Dau-
phiny to the Palatinate, after the Revocation of the Edict of Nantes,
immigrated to Pennsylvania with their widowed mother in the autumn
of 1737.

the Hoeths, the Hoffmans, the Hueds, the Kunk-
els, the Schielses, the Serfasses, the Sylvases, and the
Wicsers, all from Contented Valley; the Culvers,
and the Joneses from McMichael's Creek; the
Brewsters, the Countrymans and the Hillmans, from
Dansbury (but last from 'Sopus), and many others,
whose names in questionable orthography have been
preserved for us and remotest posterity by some
painstaking recorder of those stirring times.

In this way, during the winter of 1755 and 1756,
did The Rose exchange the character of an inn, for
that of a city of refuge. But it was also for a
time a military post, and suffered from military
occupation. This occupation fell in the interval
between the 26th of November, 1755, and the 20th
of February, 1756, and some of its incidents are
the following :

In the evening of the aforementioned 26th of
November, a company of Saucon rangers, in command of Capt. Laubach, halted at the inn, and
bivouacked for the night. Having scoured the neighboring woods next day, on receiving intelligence of
the enemy's presence in the gap of the mountain,
they broke camp at dusk, and when the moon had
risen, set out in pursuit. Meanwhile, two detachments of mounted men had arrived. These, however, failed to recognize any necessity for their
presence, and so, after having dined, departed. On

the 14th of December, Capt. Solomon Jennings*
and Capt. Doll, each with a company passed The
Rose en route for the scene of the late disaster at
Hoeth's, under orders to search for and bury the dead.
Five days later, on their return from this dangerous
anabasis, they posted Lieut. Brown with eighteen men
at the inn, for the present defence of the Moravian
settlements; and that very night, there were indica-
tions of savages lying perdu within gunshot of its
doors. Capt. Craig, at the head of a detachment
of Ulster Scots from their seats on the Calisuck,
arrived on the 21st, in order to assure himself of
the safety of his Moravian neighbors, who, it was
rumored, had been cut off by the enemy. Next followed Capts. Trump's and Aston's companies of
Provincials from the seat of justice in a remote
corner of the county, nearest the Jerseys,—their desti-

---

*The same Solomon Jennings, who, at sunrise on the 19th of Sep-
tember 1737, had set out with Edward Marshall and James Yeates
from John Chapman's corner at Wrightstown, to walk for a wager,
and to walk off land for the Penns; but who, on arriving at a point
two miles north from the Tohickon, about eleven o'clock of that
memorable morning, desisted from the contest. Falling back into the
curious crowd that followed in the wake of the three walkers, Jennings
parted company at the Fords of Lehigh, striking into the path that
led to his farm lying two miles higher up on the south bank of the
river. He deceased on the 17th of February, 1757, and his grave is
pointed out to this day near the site of the old homestead, on land
that in 1736 had been included in the Proprietaries' Manor of Fermor,
or The Drylands.

nation being Smithfield, and their errand the erection
of a block-house.   This was on the 26th of December, and the last movement of the military past
The Rose in 1755.

But in 1756, the halls of the hostelry again
echoed the tramp of martial feet, during the occupation of the Nazareth tract by Capt. Isaac Wayne
of Franklin's command, between the 5th and the
15th days of January.   "You are upon your return
from Depui's," writes the sage to his Captain, " to
halt with your company at Nazareth, and there to
remain till further orders, taking care all the while
to keep your men in good order, and to post them
in such a manner as most effectually to guard and
secure that place against any attack.   Furthermore,
you are to inform the men of your company that
they shall receive a reward from the Government
of forty pieces of eight for every Indian they shall
kill and scalp in any action they may have with
them, which I hereby promise to pay upon pro-
ducing the scalps."   In the ensuing weeks, there
was constant intercourse between Nazareth and the
men of war in Smithfield, detachments of Trump's
men coming down from Fort Hamilton to convoy
supplies of bread, baked stately in the large family
oven on the Barony, to their hungry comrades.
But the 17th of February, was, perhaps, the most
memorable day in the history of the military oc-

cupation of The Rose, and in the experience of Albrecht Klotz, its sorely-tried landlord; for on that day he was necessitated to billet sixty soldiers at Nazareth, who had been clamorous for bed and board at the already crowded inn. What was the occasion of this conflux of the sons of Mars has not yet transpired; but hereafter their calls at The Rose became less frequent, and gradually, though not uninterruptedly, its history returned into the peaceful channel in which it had flowed in the days of John F. Schaub and Divert Mary, his wife.

On the 5th of April, 1756, Andrew Schober, (born in November of 1710, near Ollmutz, in Moravia,) mason, and Hedwig Regina, his wife, were installed at The Rose, as successors to Albrecht and Margaret Klotz. The worthy couple had been brought over in the "Little Strength," Capt. Nicholas Garrison, commander, in November of 1743, and were among the first Moravians settled at Nazareth. In the second week of their novitiate a very destructive hail-storm swept over a belt of country in North-ampton, including the Rose-farm,—and, as the meteorological display set in from the north, the unshuttered lights in the gable, looking to that cardinal point of the compass, were completely wrecked. Hartmann and Catharine Verdries suc-ceeded Christian and Anna Stotz at the head of the bureau of agriculture on the fourth day of June, and not three months after this change, Mr. Schober retired from the inn. He resumed his trowel, assisted in pointing the walls of Nazareth Hall which he had in part erected, removed to Bethlehem, superintended the erection of the buckwheat mill;* and deceased at that place in July of 1792. Gottlieb, a son, born at Bethlehem in 1756, removed to Bethabara, North Carolina, in his boyhood, and deceased at Salem, in that state, in 1838. The late Samuel L. Shober, of the firm of Shober & Bunting, of Philadelphia, was a grandson of Andrew Schober of The Rose.

Thus we have come to the administration of Hartmann Verdries, and Catharine his faithful wife. Of it we know the following:

On the 20th of August, 1756, articles of agreement were drawn up and executed by George Klein, of Bethlehem, yeoman, in behalf of the Moravian

---

* The buckwheat mill at Bethlehem, built in 1765 and 1766, was the master-piece of an ingenious millwright, Christian Christensen, by name. It was originally a combination of mills, there being works for grinding flax seed and pressing oil, for peeling barley, spelt and millet, for splitting peas, for stamping and rubbing hemp, and for grinding oat meal, and bark for the tannery. Subsequently there was a snuff mill inserted, and a run of stones for buckwheat. The buckwheat flour gradually gained an enviable reputation for quality, whereupon "Bethlehem Buckwheat Flour," was annually thrown into the market in quantities which far exceeded the working capacity of the modest mill in any one season.

Society, of the one part, and Hartmann Verdries, last from the same place, miller, of the other part, in virtue of which agreement the latter assumed the responsibilities of landlord at The Rose, in tenancy under the former. Hence it was in order, that the license for the year ending with the 18th day of June, 1758, as well as the licenses for all other years pending the duration of said covenant should have been granted to Mr. Klein. The above specified license read thus:

"At a Court of General Quarter Sessions of the Peace held "at Easton, for the County of Northampton, the 21st day of "June, 1757, upon the petition of George Klein for a license to "sell beer and cyder by small measure in the township of Plain- "field, the said Court do allow and license the said George Klein "to sell beer and cyder by small measure, until the 18th day of "June next ensuing,—he observing the laws and ordinances of "this Province, which are and shall be made relating to retailers "of beer and cyder by small measure."

From the tenor of this license, it is inferable that a restriction had been laid by some one and for some reason not yet ascertained, upon the sale at The Rose of beverages indicating by hydrometric measurement a percentage of alcohol greater than is ordinarily present in either beer or cider.

Mr. Verdries, the new landlord at our inn, is a personage of some celebrity in early Moravian history. We find him superintending 'The Crown,' (that stood in Saucon township, opposite Bethlehem,) in November of 1747, a date which carries us back to almost fabulous times. There and then he associated with men like Anthony Gilbert, Jost Vollert, and Adam Schaus. Next he was appointed miller at the Friedensthal mill,* which ground its first grist on the 20th of August, 1750,—and subsequently at the Bethlehem mill, which went up in flames in a green old age in January of 1869.

---

* In January of 1750, the Moravians commenced the erection of a grist-mill for the convenience of their people at Nazareth, on a newly purchased parcel of land, watered by a branch of Lefevre's Creek (now the Bushkill), touching the Barony on the northeast, and adjacent to lands of Johannes Lefevre. It was part of a great tract of 5,000 acres granted by William Penn in October of 1681 to Lawrence Growdon, then of the parish of St. Austell, in the hundred of Powder, County of Cornwall. By him it was conveyed in 1707 to his grandson Lawrence Growdon, Jr., then of the parish of St. Merryn, in the hundred of Pyder, County of Cornwall. Growdon, Jr., conveyed 550 acres of this great tract to William Allen, of Philadelphia, merchant, in August of 1740, and from Allen, the above mentioned parcel of 324 acres, "situate on branches of Lehietan," was purchased by Henry Antes, for the use of the Moravians. In April of 1751, the improvement (up to that time called simply "the new plantation on the kill,") received the name of Friedensthal. It was stockaded in the summer of 1756 with a large but slight stockade, about 400 feet one way, and 250 the other, with log-houses at the corners for bastions. In 1767 the Moravians let, and in 1771 they disposed of the property. On the erection of the present stone mill (Mann's Mill) by Mr. Jacob Eyerly in 1796, its predecessor was converted into a dwelling, which, it is said, was demolished about 1835, its stones and timbers in part being conveyed to Stockertown, and there built up a second time into a mill.

Thence he was summoned to The Rose, over whose destinies he presided for upwards of three years. Some of the facts and incidents belonging to this eventful triennium are the following:

Among the refugees from Smithfield, residing at Nazareth, was one Francis Jones, who had fled with the Culvers, on the 11th of December, 1755. His daughter Polly, as is well known, united with the Moravians, and was thereupon admitted into the Single Sisters' House, at Bethlehem. Jones was an inmate of The Rose as late as the 17th of August, 1756. Returning to Smithfield, he entered the Province service, and in January of 1758 we find him in Capt. Nelson's command, posted at Dietz's* near the Wind Gap.

On the 31st December, 1756 there were thirteen souls billeted at The Rose and in a small log

---

* Like many other German names occurring in colonial records, this one of *Dietz* is almost completely masked in the orthography it has received at English hands. It is variously written *Teets*, ("Ensign Sterling with eleven men posted at Wind Gap, Teets' house"—*Deedts* ("Capt. Garraway with twenty-seven men at Deedts' house")—and *Teads* ("Lieut. Hyndshaw at Teads' block-house.") Lewis Gordon of Easton, who in December of 1763 was in command of an independent company, was ordered by the Governor to take post at *Hellers, late Teets' Gap.* It was therefore about 1760, that the Hellers came into possession of the well known tavern-stand in Plainfield township, south of the Gap, on the old Wilkesbarre turnpike, (now Stotz's)—which for almost a full century bore their name.

house on the farm. Ten of these were refugees
from Allemængel, on the confines of Egypt. In
addition to one Gottlieb Demuth's entire family,
there were several Volcks,—among these David Volck.
It was he who in 1760 swept chimneys on the
Barony; but growing inconveniently corpulent, after
having initiated several boys into the mysteries of the
black art, he was advised to resign in their favor.

At seven o'clock on the morning of the 5th of
July, 1757, the remains of Susan Wickel, maid-ser-
vant at Mr. Verdries', were conveyed under an armed
escort from The Rose to the old graveyard in the
woods, for burial.

In the next place it behooves us to advert briefly
to two phenomena of celestial origin which were
observed at The Rose, as well as elsewhere, in the
summer of 1757. The one was a total eclipse of
the moon on the 30th of July; the other a total
eclipse of the sun on the 14th of August following. Pursuant to orders from headquarters, Mr.
Verdries took the precaution on the last mentioned
day to house the cattle in his keeping, before the ob-
scuration should have shrouded them, their instincts,
and all things else in bewildering darkness. But the
patriarch of the herd, too old to be lured into durance
by the sprinkling of salt, continued at large, heighten-
ing by his lamentations the terrors of the awful gloom.

It is generally known that Owen Rice, who

had arrived on the "Catharine," Capt. Thomas Gladman, commander, in June of 1742, and who returned to England in 1754, (he deceased at Gomersal, wapentake of Morley, West Riding of the County of York, in 1788), set out the first orchard at Nazareth. This he did in April of 1745. Others emulating him in so important and so entirely disinterested a labor of love, the farms on the tract were ere long embowered in apple trees— and the trees thriving, cider was pressed on the Barony for the first time in August of 1755. In September of 1757 the trees hung full,—all grafted fruit—and there was promise of a large ingathering. But the apples were ripening in lawless times, and it soon appeared that unless some positive means were taken to check the depredations committed on these Hesperian gardens, little of the goodly yield would fall to the share of those to whom it rightly belonged. Hence the following " Caution " was displayed in the tap-room at The Rose.

" This is to notify whom it may concern, that in these uncer-
" tain times, the watch will set their dogs on, or, if need be,
" fire upon all persons, whether white or Indian, who shall be
" found trespassing in the orchards at Nazareth, Friedensthal, The
" Rose, Gnadenthal and Christian's Spring."

It was argued that the warning would be most likely to catch the eyes of offenders at The Rose; but to make a sure thing of it, duplicates of the ordinance were posted at the mill, and in the smith-shop at the Spring.

There is a waif of Provincial history, which claims our consideration at this point of the narrative. On the 16th of September of the above mentioned year 1757, while one Joseph Keller (who brought his butter to the Bethlehem market as early as 1746, receipting payment for the same with a boldly drawn J. K.) was assisting his neighbors in plowing, three Indians surprised his farm-house, which stood about five miles north by east from Nazareth in Plain-field township, and carried off his wife and sons. Intelligence of this irruption of Ishmaelites having been duly brought to Bethlehem, and communicated to Tadeuskundt, the Delaware king, he, the king, despatched three of his Indians and two whites to Keller's, to ascertain whether any of his subjects had been concerned in the high-handed outrage. As their way led past The Rose, Justice Horsfield of Beth-lehem very considerately furnished the five with a curt letter of recommendation to its worthy host, as follows:

"To Mr. Hartmann Verdries, at The Rose, near Nazareth:

"Pray let the bearers, Jacob Volck and Levi Jung, and three "Indians have such refreshments as is needful; but don't let them "have much liquor, and send me an account of what they receive "that I may charge it.

HORSFIELD."

BETHLEHEM, 18th September, 1757.

Thus the Province became indebted to our inn to the amount of ten shillings and nine pence,— the voucher for said indebtedness being couched in these words :

" Province of Pennsilvania, Dr:

" To Sundries delivered at Nazareth Tavern to Jacob Volck, " Lewis Jung and three Indians, who was sent by Tadeuskundt " to Joseph Keller's place to satisfy him of the truth of Keller's " wife and children being taken captive, viz. :"

1757.		£.	s.	d.
"Sept. 18.	To victuals and drink, . .		4	10
"	½ peck of oats, .			6
" 19.	" victuals and drink, . .		4	11
"	½ peck of oats, . . .			6
			10	9

HARTMANN VERDRIES."

Altogether different in character, though forsooth a record of blood, is the following item of particular history. In December of 1757 the residents of the adjacents of Nazareth were duly notified, that such of them as desired to be bled, (it was in a time when venesection was in vogue) should no longer repair to Bethlehem to Dr. Otto, nor to the room of Joseph Miller, practitioner of physic, in Nazareth Hall,* as had heretofore been done to the annoyance of the household;—but instead, should rendezvous at The Rose, where said Joseph Miller, practitioner of physic, would within certain hours

---

* Nazareth Hall, designed for the residence of Count Zinzendorf, was brought under roof in less than five months, to wit: in the interval between the 3d of May and the 24th of September, 1755. As at the erection of the Tower of Babel, so at the building of this goodly structure, the workmen spoke in diverse tongues, there being Englishmen, Welshmen, Frenchmen, Germans, Bohemians, Danes and a native of the Guinea Coast among the industrious company. But there was no discord, nor did any casualty attend the rapid construction of the fortress-like walls, braced with ponderous girders of heart-of-oak. The Indian war, however, interrupted the work in the autumn of 1755, so that a full year elapsed before the completion of the chapel, which was dedicated on the 13th November, 1756. In this chapel the Moravians at Nazareth worshipped for almost a century.

But Count Zinzendorf failed to visit his American brethren a second time, and the house was accordingly converted to other uses. On the 27th of November, 1756, David and Regina Heckewelder (the parents of John Heckewelder, missionary among the Indians), and George Volck and his family, refugees from Allemaengel, occupied rooms in the unfinished building. They were the first tenants. The apartments on the second floor having been completed in April of 1757, Joseph Miller, M. D. and Verona his wife (imported in the Irene in May of 1749), took possession of several, and on the 30th of June, Bishop Spangenberg and his wife Mary, of others. Gov. Denny rode up from Easton on the 19th October, 1758, specially to inspect the majestic structure. A school for sons of Moravian parents was commenced in the house in June of 1759. The "Boarding School for Young Gentlemen at Nazareth Hall," dates back to the 3d of October, 1785.

on certain days of every month, give audience in the "great room," to as many as desired to consult him professionally in the vital matter of venesection.

On the 12th of April, 1758, the inn was in imminent danger of being consumed by a "bush-fire," which swept down from the adjacent barrens, under a stiff north-wester;—and on the 28th of the month, we find the brothers Francis and George Clevel, with their families, a fourth time refugees, under the shelter of its protecting wings.

Hartmann and Catharine Verdries and their infant daughter, Ann Rosina, were the sole occupants of the house on the last day of 1758. Three months later they closed their administration of its concerns. Of Mr. Verdries' subsequent history, we know nothing, save that in 1760 he was a second time miller at Friedensthal; that while there his son Lewis was born, 17th January, 1760, and that a grandson, Peter Verdries, was an eminent classical teacher in .Philadelphia between 1815 and 1825.

The sixth landlord at The Rose in the succession, was Ephraim Culver, late from Lower Smithfield, miller,—but a native of Connecticut,—having been born on the 30th July, 1717, in the town of Lebanon, in that Government. Mr. Culver was installed at the inn, as near as we can ascertain, about the time of the vernal equinox of 1759.

Together with his wife Elizabeth, m. n. Smith, whom he had married in "The Oblong," he conducted the affairs of the now historic house for almost six long years. Of his life antecedent to that epoch, it affords us much pleasure, in view of his importance in the annals of The Rose, to be able to state the following particulars. In 1753 he left Connecticut, removed with his family to Smithfield, and settled upon a small glebe he had purchased of Daniel Broadhead. On this site, now in the centre of the borough of Strouds-burgh, he erected a grist-mill, (its wheel was turned by the waters of McMichael's Creek) and looked forward, no doubt, to years of peaceful industry—and then retirement from business and rest in the evening of life. But this prospect was rudely marred when Mr. Culver on the 11th of December, 1755, saw a cloud of smoke ascend from the site of his house and mill, as he was fleeing with wife and children before the destroying Indians. With others of his neighbors he sought a friendly asylum at Nazareth. There, ere long, he united with the Moravians—there he indentured his son Ephraim (who deceased at Schoeneck in September of 1804) to the miller,—there he lost his daughter Sarah in May of 1756 (she lies buried in the old "Indian Graveyard,")—and there was his home until he was tendered the position of landlord at "The Crown," in October of 1756. Mr. Culver's eventful administration of the affairs of that ancient hostelry, fills a leaf in the book of Colonial history. It fell in those years in which Tadeuskundt and his hangers-on were constantly on the wing between Fort Allen and Easton, and Easton and Fort Allen—playing at "toss and catch" with Governor Denny and his men of state, or beguiling them at numberless treaties and conferences by soft words and the music of Indian oratory, to hope for peace,—when there was war. And ever and anon would these ghastly, gaunt and ominous birds light in a flock at The Crown, invade the sanctity of the landlord's private apartments, as well as the tap-room and the larder, and clamor for victuals and drink in guttural Minsi and harsh-sounding Nanticoke. They would come at all hours of the day, and even the midnight air was known to sound with the rushing of their wings. Thus the landlord was sorely tried. But he found his barbaric customers as full of whims also as they were importunate. There was no compound or decoction current in that day among the whites, but what was called for by these thirsty Indians. Witness the unreasonable demands of Peepy and Montour, two runners, who, before setting out on a distant mission in January of 1757, indulged in diverse pints and half-pints of wine, in quarts of cider, in

drams and hot drams, in mim* and in rum,—and
departed only after having come into possession of
"a quart of rum and ye bottle." Such was the school
in which Mr. Culver was disciplined in the lesser
arts of his calling; while occasional intercourse
with men like Conrad Weisser, Capt. Jacob Arndt,
Hugh Crawford, and George Croghan,—and with
Moses Tattamy, Paxanosa, and French Margaret,—
Indian kings and queens, furnished him with a
knowledge of the world and mankind, such as
enabled him to conduct the affairs of The Rose
acceptably during the six years of his incumbency.
From its unusual length it may very naturally be
argued, that its current flowed smoothly in a channel unruffled by rift or riffle. This was the case,
save in the autumn of 1763, when a second war
with the Indians was imminent, and cismontane
Northampton again suffered from hostile invasion.

In April of 1763, William Edmonds, a native
of Coleford in the parish of Newland, hundred of
St. Briavell's, county of Gloucester, leather-dresser,

---

* Mim, abbreviated from mimbo—a drink prepared from rum, water
and loaf-sugar, as appears from the following "rates in Taverns," fixed
by the Justices of York County, Pennsylvania, in January of 1752,
"for the protecting of travellers from the extortions of inn-holders."

    1 qt. mimbo, made of West India rum and loaf, . . 10 d.

    1 "   "   "   " New England rum and loaf, . 9

    Carter & Glossbrenner's History of York County, York, 1834.

(since 1742 attached to the Moravians), became an inmate of The Rose, prior to taking charge of a store which was in course of erection a few rods south from the inn on the Minisink road. On the completion of this place of traffic the hostelry assumed the character of a mart; but especially in the interval between 1765 and 1772, when the Moravian Indians from Wyalusing (Bradford county), and others from places as remote as Sheshequin, Shamunk and Owege, came to the store to barter skins and wooden ware for strouds and half-thicks, and powder and lead. Mr. Edmonds relinquished his position at The Rose in 1772—was appointed shop-keeper in the village of Nazareth, and deceased there in September of 1786.

Several allusions having been made in the course of this narrative to the Rose-farm, it may be well to dispossess the reader of any erroneous preconception in reference to its extent. It was never more than a small glebe, with sufficiency of arable land and meadow to supply the house with bread and a few cows with pasture. Would any one, however, be fully informed in respect to the details of its agricultural department, he may consult the annual assessments of the inn for County and Province taxes still extant, or the following inventory. This affords us also a glance into the very penetralia of the goodly house.

INVENTORY OF THE STOCK IN THE ROSE INN.

31st May, 1764, amounting to 64 £ 15 s. 7 d.

	s.	d.	£.	s.	d.	£.	s.	d.
20 bu. of rye, . . @	2	9	1	15	—			
15 bu. of oats, . . . @	2		1	10	—			
2 bu. of buckwheat, . @	1	8		3	4			
150 lbs. of pork, . . . @		6	3	15	—			
10 lbs. of butter, @		6	—	5	—			
15 lbs. of tallow, . . @		7	—	8	9			
6 lbs. of lard, . . . @		6	—	3	—			
32 galls. of soft soap, . @		8	1	1	4			
10 lbs. of cheese, . . @		9		7	6			
						9	8	11
2 hogsheads of cider, . @	30		3	—	—			
10 galls. of Teneriffe,* @	5	6	2	15	—			
28 galls. Barbadoes Rum, @	4	1	5	14	4			
23 galls. of New Eng-								
land Rum, . . . @	3		3	9	—			
15 galls. of metheglin, . @	1			15	—			
						15	13	4
17 yds. linen of flax, . @	3		2	11	—			
10 yds. linen of tow, . @	1	8		16	8			
2¾ yds. of cloth, . . @	3	6		9	7½			
Yarn, ...				2	6			
						3	19	9½

* Philip C. Bader, (who deceased at Nazareth in March of 1797) in a rhythmical narrative descriptive of the incidents of his voyage to America in the autumn of 1751, sings at large of the peak of Teyde on Teneriffe, in the shadow of whose cone ripened the generous wine that was quaffed at The Rose.

	£	s.	d.	£	s.	d.
½ load of hay, ...		19	—			
3 cows, ... @ £4 10s.	13	10	—			
2 calves, . . . @ 10s.	1	—	—			
2 hogs, ...	1					
				16	9	
	£	s.	d.			
½ lb of powder, ...		1	6			
1 iron kettle received for a debt, . .	1	2	6			
Sundry small outstanding debts, ...	11	2	7			
Cash on hand, ...	4	8	—			
				16	14	7
	£	s.	d.			
2 acres sowed in oats, . @ 12s.	1	4	—			
4 bu. of oats sowed in, @ 2s.		8	—			
¼ acre sowed in flax, ...		5	—			
¼ bu. of flax seed, ...		1	3			
½ acre of Indian corn, ...		12	—			
				2	10	3
				64	15	7

The 4th of April, 1765, was perhaps the most memorable day in the incumbency of Ephraim Culver at the inn. In the forenoon of that day the precincts of the house were suddenly thronged by a motley crowd of Indians,—men, women, and children, whose appearance and equipments indicated them to be a people migrating in search of new homes. They were the Moravian Indians, lately returned from confinement in the Barracks at Philadelphia,—en route for Wyalusing. Thus far they had journeyed under escort, and protected by the strong arm of the law; and here they took sad leave of the people among whom their lot had been cast for upwards of twenty years.

Two weeks after this event, Mr. Culver retired from The Rose, having accepted the appointment of landlord at The Crown, for a second time. This he managed until the decease of his wife in 1771. In April of 1772, he became a resident of Schoeneck, and soon after married Mary C. Claus. Mr. Culver deceased at Bethlehem in March of 1775.

John and Mary Catharine Lischer were installed at The Rose on the 20th of April 1765, and administered its concerns until the 30th of March 1772. Mr. Lischer was the last in the succession of its landlords. With his retirement on the 30th of March 1772, it ceased to be an inn; for in 1771 the house and its adjacents, (which at that time embraced a tract of two hundred and forty acres, touching the head-line of the Barony and situate in Plainfield township,) were sold by the Moravian Society to Dorst Alleman,—a native of the Canton of Berne, Switzerland, but prior to 1761 an inhabitant of Lancaster County, yeoman,—and confirmed to him by indenture bearing date of 17th October, 1783.

It was Alleman, therefore, who plucked the rose from the old ancestral tree.

He and Verona his wife, took possession on the
1st of April, 1772. Yet even in its decadence the
goodly house was honored; for in September
of 1772, Governor John Penn, son of Richard
Penn, son of William Penn by Hannah Callowhill,
passed a week under its hospitable roof, while re-
laxing from the cares of state in shooting grouse
on the neighboring barrens. Mr. Watson tells us
that the Governor "was in person of the middle
size, reserved in manners and very near sighted;"
whence it is inferable that the slaughter of grouse, as
far as he was individually concerned, was only moder-
ate; nevertheless, his Honor, being an English gen-
tleman of the old school, may have relished the sport
and have been benefited, too, by the country air and
country living.

Dorst Alleman deceased at his mansion, late The
Rose, in March of 1803.

Benedict Benade* of Plainfield township, painter
and potter, sole executor of the last will and tes-
tament of Dorst Alleman, confirmed the Rose tract to
Mattes Alleman, of the aforesaid township, yeoman,
only son and residuary legatee of the aforesaid
Dorst, by indenture bearing date of 28th December

---

* Benedict Benade, horn in Upper Lusatia in September of 1752, immigrated in 1793—married Elizabeth, the eldest daughter of Dorst Alleman, and deceased in Filetown in 1841.

1803: Mattes Alleman deceased in December of 1819. His executors, Molly Alleman and John A. Edmonds,* some time after, exposing seventy-eight acres of the original tract (including The Rose) for sale at vendue or public outcry, these were purchased by George Gold, of Bushkill township, yeoman, for thirteen hundred and twelve dollars and sixty-seven cents, and confirmed to him by indenture bearing date of 17th April, 1826.

George Gold and Rosina his wife, conveyed the premises to David Gold, of Bushkill township, yeoman, in February of 1831. By David Gold and Mary his wife, they were conveyed to Gideon Haupt, of Bushkill township, yeoman, in April of 1840.

Mrs. Louisa Reinheimer, a daughter of Gideon Haupt, the present holder, came into possession of the property in April of 1865.

In conclusion, we would state, that in the summer of 1858 the olden hostelry was demolished; but the gables of the tenant-house which stands on its site, are covered with boards that survived the wreck;—sole remaining, but alas! withered leaves shed from the Red Rose that once bloomed on the Barony of Nazareth.

---

* A son of William Edmonds. Born on Long Island in May of 1743, deceased in Plainfield township in April of 1824.

Our personal recollections of the historic house extend over the period of time usually allotted to two generations of mortal men. In that long interval it suffered no perceptible change. It failed even to grow older. From first to last it was the same tall, spectral-looking mansion, clad in a coat of faded Spanish brown;—standing no longer on the great highway between the capital of a Province and its frontiers, but on a by-way in a secluded and forsaken corner of what was once part of the Barony of Nazareth. Its barns were rickety, its cider-press was ancient, its fruit-trees were mossy; and yet from first to last they suffered no perceptible change—they failed to grow older. In men's minds the house was vaguely associated with a long-past Indian age. They spoke of its having been beleaguered, and pointed to the knot-holes in the shrunken weather-boarding as the work of balls from savage rifles. They spoke of its precincts as having been the homes of successive generations of red men, and testified to their presence with arrow-heads and tomahawks of stone, gleaned from the neighboring fields. And there were even some who stated that the old Red Rose had been planted on haunted ground; and down to the year of its demolition, there might be heard in the time of the September moon, as soon as its beams began to silver the veil of mist that hangs nightly over the milkhouse in the meadow, the voice of a horseman on the upland, chiding his loitering steed in an unknown tongue;—it being the spirit of the bold Minsi from Peoqueahlin, carrying off the stolen daughter of Tagh-tapasset, the Delaware king of Welagamika.*

Here end the chronicles of The Rose.

* The name of the Indian town that stood on the Barony of Nazareth, on its first occupation by the Moravians, in the spring of 1740. There is a draft in the room of the Moravian Historical Society, entitled "A Draft of Nazareth and adjacent lands," drawn in March of 1757, on which the site of the old Indian town is marked on the south side of the run irrigating the meadows that lie north by east from the "Whitefield House,"—perhaps thirty rods east from the "old Minisink road." The word Welagamika is compounded from *whe-lik*, and *ha-ga-mi-ka*, words in the Unami Delaware, signifying, *the best* of *tillable land.*

The Old Inn at Nazareth.

1771.

The house in which we are met on this memorial day, comes to us from that period in the history of the Moravians, in which they began to assimilate with the other elements of the population that had taken root in the Province, and that were crowding them in their exclusive settlements. The Economy at Nazareth was dissolved in 1764. This led to many changes; the most important of which were the concentration of their people on fewer farms, and the subsequent founding of the village, now the borough, of Nazareth. This was laid out on a parcel of six hundred acres of land, situate between what was henceforth called Old Nazareth (its gigantic tile-roofed barn stands to the present day)—and Nazareth Hall, in January of 1771. The first dwelling was completed before the close of that year. But a village without an inn, it was argued, would be Hamlet without the ghost, and ill equipped for the struggle for existence, and hence preparations were made in due time for the erection of the indispensable appendage. These were so far completed as to admit of the first layer of well-hewn hickory

logs being put down, on the 5th day of August of
the last mentioned year.   Day by day the work of
blocking-up progressed under the hands of the
young men from the Economy at Christian's
Spring;* the house was brought under roof, and
during the winter of 1771 and 1772, the details of
its interior were developed in accordance with the
architect's design.   In the spring of the last mentioned year it was occupied.   But before passing
on to a review of the administration of its affairs,
we would submit the following statement of the cost
at which the hostelry was erected.   It is dated 31st
January, 1772, and reads thus :

	£.	s.	d.
I. For work done by the Economy at Christian's Spring, amounting to,	136	2	11
II. For work done by, and board provided for workmen, from elsewhere, amounting to,	209	11	10
For bricks &c.,	124	3	6
Total,	469	18	3

The public house at Nazareth, erected and completed at this outlay of pounds, shillings and pence,
Pennsylvania currency, is described by a contempo-
rary writer as having been "a rather murky-looking

---

* This Economy dated back to December of 1749.   It was dissolved
in 1796.

tenement;" but in course of time it was improved, enlarged, and ultimately renovated. In fact it passed through all the phases incident to inns that revolve acceptably around the patronage and favor of a fickle but discriminating public.

On the 30th of March, 1772, John Lischer, a native of Hilzhof, margraviate of Wittgenstein, farmer, and Mary Catharine, m. n. Loesch, a daughter of George Loesch of Tulpehocken, his wife, were´ installed at the inn, in the capacity of landlord and landlady. Mr. Lischer had immigrated early in life, and settled in Oley. From there he removed to Bethlehem in 1743. In October of 1753, he accompanied a colony of young men, sént thence to make a settlement on the newly purchased "Moravian tract," in western North Carolina. We next find him discharging the duties of an express-rider between Bethlehem and that distant point. One October morning in 1758, while Mr. Lischer and a comrade were returning from Philadelphia, whither they had been to market, they and their team were impressed in the Province service; and so . it came to pass that before the close of a week, he had loaded up salt, and was en route for Rays-town (Bedford), where Genl. Forbes was collecting a formidable force for the expulsion of the French from the country of the Ohio. Mr. Lischer married in 1759. In 1762, he was appointed landlord at

The Crown, and subsequently, as has been stated, at The Rose. His wife was yet in her 'teens, when far into the night of the 29th of May, 1745, she assisted her mother in Tulpehocken in finishing a tent for Bishop Spangenberg, who was on the morrow to set out for Onondaga. Having been reared in the school of Moravian housewifery, she was privileged to lay the first stone in that pile which has since been growing and which commemorates the good cheer that has always been dispensed at the Nazareth Inn.

Mr. Lischer deceased in May of 1782, and was buried in the beautiful cemetery on the hill, which his hands had assisted in adorning.

John Michael Moehring, born in September of 1739, at Hirschberg in Voigtland, farmer, imported in the good ship Hope, Capt. Christian Jacobsen, in September of 1761, was the second landlord of the inn. He succeeded Mr. Lischer in March of 1775; but finding the duties of his position too onerous for one, he wisely sought a helpmate, and choosing Elizabeth Rauschenberger, he was married to her on the 30th of April following.

Two days before that important event in his life, an affair of importance in the life of the American people had occurred at Lexington. This and its long and tedious chain of consequences, link for link, afforded motives of conversation at the Naza-

reth Inn (as well as at all other inns) for the re-
mainder of Mr. Moehring's administration; and
when he retired from the house at whose head he
had stood for nine eventful years, it no longer owed
allegiance to King George the Third, and the
Province had become a free and independent State.

Mr. Moehring deceased at Nazareth in April of
1796. He left no issue.

On the 19th of March, 1784, Owen Rice, and Elizabeth, née Eyerly, his wife, assumed the management
of the inn. Mr. Rice was a son of the Owen
Rice who had set out the first orchard on the
Barony, and was born in the city of New York, in
August of 1751. During his incumbency the house
gradually acquired a wide-spread reputation, as on the
3d of October, 1785, a boarding-school for young
gentlemen was commenced in Nazareth Hall; and
in the inn its visiting patrons found a temporary
home.

Mr. Rice deceased at Bethlehem, in August of
1820.

The fourth landlord in the succession was John
Kremser, a native of Nazareth, but at the time of
his appointment, a member of the Economy at
Christian's Spring. Having married Ann Mary
Peischer in March of 1790, he thereupon under-
took the control of the house, and remained its re-
sponsible head for upwards of ten years. But in

that interval he lost his wife. He next married Ann Sybilla Beck, in February of 1793. Mr. Kremser deceased at Bethlehem, in November of 1823.

John Lewis Roth, Mr. Kremser's successor, conducted the affairs of the inn, in the interval between October of 1800, and October of 1808. Mr. Roth was the first child of white parents born within the borders of the state of Ohio, he seeing the light of day on the 4th of July, 1773, at the Gnadenhutten mission, on the Tuscarawas branch of the Muskingum. In 1785 he was a pupil at Nazareth Hall. His subsequent career is partially obscure; but he was a resident of the Moravian settlement at Hope, Warren County, New Jersey, when he was tendered the position of landlord at Nazareth. Mr. Roth deceased at Bath, Northampton County, Pa., in September of 1841.

On the 27th October, 1808, Joseph Rice, a son of the third landlord, and Ann Salome, a daughter of the missionary John Heckewelder, his wife, were installed at the inn. They conducted its concerns for upwards of two years. Mr. Rice deceased at Bethlehem, in 1827.

John S. Haman and Sarah, m. n. Schmick, his wife, were host and hostess at our inn, between June of 1811, and March of 1836, presiding over its fortunes, therefore, for almost a quarter of a century. Hence Mr. Haman was the landlord *par excellence* of the Nazareth Inn. He deceased at that place in February of 1866, in the seventy-ninth year of his age.

The landlords of this house up to 1836, without exception, were members of the Moravian Church. During the ensuing sixteen years, however, it was let to gentlemen who were not members of that Society, and in 1835, it was sold to Peter Best.

William Craig was landlord between April of 1836 and April of 1842. Him followed Daniel Riegel, who resigned in favor of Peter Best, in April of 1852. Best, as has been stated, bought the house. Between 1854 and 1868, Edward Siegfried, Henry Whitesell, Richard Whitesell, Garnet and Leidy, and George Hager, followed in rapid succession. And finally, in the last mentioned year, the old Nazareth Inn was taken by Jesse Billheimer, the present popular incumbent.

APPENDIX.

Containing notices supplementary to the preceding historical sketch.

I.

Francis and George Clevel.   Francis, the older of the two brothers, was born 27th September, 1720, at Auerbach, in Baden Durlach. While on shipboard he was redeemed by a German farmer, on whose plantation in Oley, Berks county, he passed his servitude.   Having married Salome Kichline in 1746, he disposed of his cabin set in among the Oley Hills, and with his wife and infant daughter, Magdalene, removed to the wilds of Northampton county, locating on the Lehietan, or Hakijannecke, about two miles north from Nazareth.   The site of his house is pointed out about one mile southeast from the Douglass Slate Quarry, in Bushkill township.   Here he deceased 24th January, 1798.   Three sons, John, Francis, and Nathaniel, twenty-eight grand-children and one great-grand-child survived the venerable patriarch.

George, his brother, was born 18th November, 1726, at Auerbach, and deceased at Schœneck, 6th May, 1793.   He was the father of nine sons and three daughters.   Daniel, one of the nine, and father of the aged Mr. Philip Clevel of Schœneck, was born in the Whitefield House, in February of 1756, while his parents were refugees at Nazareth.

The Moravian ministers settled at that place, preached statedly in Francis Clevel's house, on the Bushkill, in the interval between the spring of 1755 and the autumn of 1762. Subsequently, the Clevels attended divine worship in the chapel at Schœneck, and united with the Moravians. That quaint old building, high-roofed and girt with low porches, which hangs on the declivity of the hill as you go down to the Bushkill on your way to Bushkill Center, popularly called " Das Schweitzer Haus," was built by Francis Clevel, Jr., circa 1776.

II.

Ann Margaret, wife of *Albrecht Klotz,* deceased at Nazareth in June of 1758. *Lewis,* his brother, was attached to the Moravians as early as 1745, and was then a resident of Macungy, his farm lying adjacent to the Moravian property in Salisbury township. Subsequently, and for many years, Lewis Klotz was a Justice of the Peace in Northampton county. His children were placed at Moravian schools. Jasper Payne, in 1742 enrolled in the Moravian Society in London, as cheesemonger and wine-cooper, corner of Queen street and Watling street, St. Antholines,—but, in 1746, accountant for the " Bethlehem Economy," has left the following items on record. " August 11th, 1746, Lewis Klotz's child died at Herzer's last Tuesday was sevennight, being the 5th of August." And, " May 24th, 1747, Received of Lewis Klotz towards paying of his children's board and schooling :

	£.	s.	d.
3 Cows, ...	9	—	—
2 Calves, ...	—	10	—
1 Mare and a little colt with a bell			
on the mare	7	—	—
1 Cow-bell	—	5	—
	16	15	—

III.

Gottlieb Demuth was born in 1715, in Radelsdorf in Bohemia, whence he and others of his family emigrated to Saxony and became attached to the Moravians at Herrnhut. In 1736 he was sent with a colony to Georgia. In June of 1737 he came to Pennsylvania, settled first among the Metuchen Hills, and next at Bethlehem. He deceased at Schœneck in October of 1776. His house stood a short quarter of a mile south of The Rose, on the Minisink road.

IV.

The Volcks. The ancestor of the Volcks, whose family-tree, prior to 1750, overshadowed a goodly portion of Allemængel, now. Lynn township, Lehigh county, was Andries Volck, born near Worms in 1678. He and Ann Catharine his wife, and sons and daughters, belonged to a company of fifty-two German Protestants, whom, with their minister, one Joshua Kocherthal, Queen Anne was graciously pleased to send to New York and settle at her own expense, in the autumn of 1708. They pitched their tents first on Quassek creek (now Chambers' creek, near Newburg), in the Highlands, at a spot called by the Dutch "De Dans-Kammer." Thence the Volcks removed to Allemængel, circa 1735. Old Andries deceased there in September of 1747, the father of eleven children, of whom, Andrew, Charles, Jacob and George, the surviving sons, in due course of time, became the heads of prosperous families.

V.

Philip C. Bader. The cittern with which Mr. Bader (as he tells us in his miniature epic), was wont to beguile the tedious hours of long weeks at sea, may be seen in the collection of relics belonging to the Moravian Historical Society. From the father the sounding shell passed into the hands of the daughter—the same Julia Bader who, while an inmate of the Single Sisters' House at Bethlehem, assisted in embroidering a banner for Pulaski, at the time the General was recruiting his immortal legion in Northampton and Berks.

VI.

Specified account of the expenses incurred in erecting the Nazareth Inn, in 1771.

1. For work done by the Economy at Christian's Spring—viz. :

	£	s.	d.
For 509 days' carpentering, felling and squaring timber, blocking up, laying floors, &c., @ 2s. 6d.,	63	12	6
" 57 days' board for the carpenters, @ 1s. per day,	2	17	—
" 452 breakfasts and suppers, @ 7d.,	13	3	8
" hauling stone and timber,	26	4	—
" hauling 44 logs to the saw-mill,	11	—	—
" sawing,	19	5	9
	136	2	11

2. For work done by, and for board provided for workmen from elsewhere, viz. :

	£	s.	d.
For digging cellar,	5	2	6
" quarrying stone,	12	13	5
" hauling stone,	9	9	—
" hauling stone and timber,	20	18	2
" mason-work,	46	12	—
" carpentering and blocking up,	11	14	—
" hod-carriers and day-laborers,	30	—	—
" carpenters' fine work,	32	4	4½
" blacksmiths' work,	5	12	5
" board and whiskey,	35	5	6½
	209	11	10

				£	s.	d.
For 17,150 bricks, @ 30s. per m.,		.	.	25	14	6
" 8,807 feet of pine boards,	.	.	.	28	2	6
" 2 boxes of glass, .	.	.	.	8	1	—
" 2 iron stoves,	.	.	.	7	4	—
" work done at the stoves,	.	.	.	7	14	5
" 15 locks,	.	.	.	4	5	3
" hair for mortar, .	.	.	.	—	11	6
" clapboards, .	.	.	.	—	19	3
" shovels, hoes, &c.,	.	.	.	9	10	—
" logs from the woods,	.	.	.	12	3	—
" nails, .	.	.	.	19	6	1
" plank for stairway,	.	.	.	—	2	—.
				469	18	3

www.ingramcontent.com/pod-product-compliance
Lightning Source LLC
Chambersburg PA
CBHW021545270326
41930CB00008B/1374